580
LUN

Plant Life Cycles

by Julie K. Lundgren

Science Content Editor:
Kristi Lew

www.rourkepublishing.com

Science content editor: Kristi Lew

A former high school teacher with a background in biochemistry and more than 10 years of experience in cytogenetic laboratories, Kristi Lew specializes in taking complex scientific information and making it fun and interesting for scientists and non-scientists alike. She is the author of more than 20 science books for children and teachers.

www.rourkepublishing.com

Photo credits: Cover © dionisvera, beboy; Cover logo frog © Eric Pohl, test tube © Sergey Lazarev; Page 4 © Ruslan Rizvanov; Page 5 © sharon kingston; Page 6/7 © Linda Macpherson; Page 8 © de2marco; Page 9 © Anne Kitzman; Page 11 © Katrina Leigh; Page 13 © Vaclav Volrab;Page 14 © R-photos; Page 15 © Vaclav Volrab; Page 16 © Brzostowska; Page 17 © dionisvera; Page 19 © David Koscheck; Page 20 © kaczor58, Martin Novak; Page 21 © Fotofermer, kosam;

Editor: Kelli Hicks

Cover and page design by Nicola Stratford, bdpublishing.com

Library of Congress Cataloging-in-Publication Data

Lundgren, Julie K.
 Plant life cycles / Julie K. Lundgren.
   p. cm. -- (My science library)
 Includes bibliographical references and index.
 ISBN 978-1-61741-734-4 (Hard cover) (alk. paper)
 ISBN 978-1-61741-936-2 (Soft cover)
 1. Plant life cycles--Juvenile literature. I. Title.
 QK49.L865 2012
 580--dc22
                          2011003901

Rourke Publishing
Printed in the United States of America,
North Mankato, Minnesota
060711
060711CL

ROURKE
PUBLISHING

www.rourkepublishing.com - rourke@rourkepublishing.com
Post Office Box 643328 Vero Beach, Florida 32964

Table of Contents

Packet of Life........................4

Life Unfolding....................10

Flowers 16

Show What You Know.... 22

Glossary 23

Index 24

Packet of Life

Every living thing begins, can **reproduce**, and dies. In many plants, this **life cycle** begins with a seed.

Have you ever planted seeds?

A seed holds the beginnings of a plant's first **roots**, **stem**, and leaves.

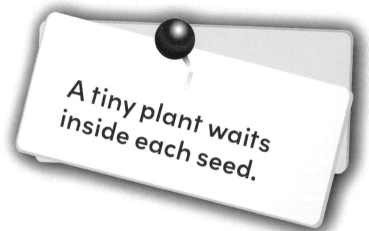

A tiny plant waits inside each seed.

A seed ready to grow.

Roots begin to grow.

Roots grow bigger.

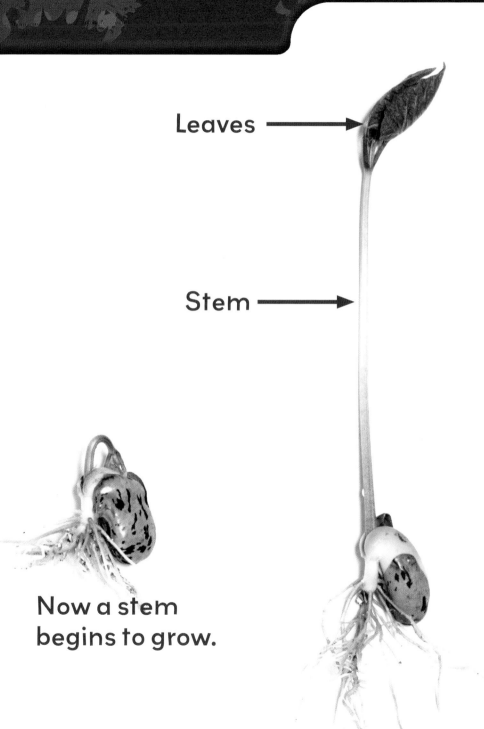

Leaves ➝

Stem ➝

Now a stem
begins to grow.

Some plants begin from a **bulb**. Bulbs grow roots, stems, and leaves, too.

An onion plant begins from a bulb.

Life Unfolding

The tiny plant grows. Roots make a strong base. They take in water and **nutrients** from the soil.

Roots grow.

The first **shoot** becomes a strong stem. The stem carries water and nutrients to the plant and holds up the leaves.

Leaves grow from plant stems.

Stem

13

Leaves use sunlight, air, and water to make food for the plant.

Leaves are food factories for plants.

Leaves

Flowers

Some plants make flowers. Plants make seeds inside their flowers.

Marigold seeds

Marigold flowers make marigold seeds.

When they are ready, some seeds fall to the ground. Animals or the wind will carry other seeds to new places to grow.

The wind blows dandelion seeds to a new place.

19

At the end of the life cycle, plants die. Their bodies **decay**. New plants will grow in their place.

Life Cycle of an Oak Tree • • • • • • • • • •

1. The acorn sprouts.

4. The tree makes flowers and acorns. After many years, the tree dies.

2. A young tree grows.

3. The tree grows bigger.

21

SHOW What You Know

1. How does each plant part help the plant grow?

2. What role do flowers play in a plant's life cycle?

3. Can you think of some plants that grow from bulbs?

Glossary

bulb (BUHLB): the part of a plant where food is stored and from which a new plant can grow

decay (dee-KAY): to break down and rot

life cycle (LIFE SY-kuhl): the never-ending process by which animals and plants begin, reproduce, and die

nutrients (NOO-tree-uhnts): minerals and other chemicals in the soil that are needed by plants to stay healthy and grow

reproduce (ree-proh-DOOS): to make more plants, often by way of seeds

roots (ROOTS): plant parts that are usually underground and take in water and nutrients for the plant to grow and stay healthy

shoot (SHOOT): a new plant stem

stem (STEM): the part of the plant that connects the roots to the leaves

Index

bulb(s) 8, 9

flowers 16, 17, 20

leaves 6, 7, 8, 12, 14

life cycle 4, 20

nutrients 10, 12

roots 6, 8, 10, 11

seed(s) 4, 5, 6, 16, 17, 18, 19

stem(s) 6, 7, 8, 12, 13

Websites

urbanext.illinois.edu

www.exploringnature.org

php?dbID=32&detID=1208

www.ftexploring.com/me/photosyn1.html

www.loc.gov/rr/scitech/mysteries/coconut.html

www.tooter4kids.com/Plants/index.htm

About the Author

Julie K. Lundgren grew up near Lake Superior where she liked to muck about in the woods, pick berries, and expand her rock collection. Her interests led her to a degree in biology. She lives in Minnesota with her family.